CASUALLY DISCUSSING THE INFINITE

STU BUCK

ILLUSTRATIONS BY PETER HALL

SNOW LEOPARD PUBLISHING

For information contact :
Snow Leopard Publishing
http://www.snowleopardpublishing.com
email: info@snowleopardpublishing.com

ISBN: 978-1-94436158-7 (paperback)
        978-1-94436159-4(hardcover)
        978-1-94436160-0(ebook)

Cover Design and Illustrations by Peter Hall

First Edition: April 2017

10 9 8 7 6 5 4 3 2 1

TABLE OF CONTENTS

the jackdaws...

...clattered into the pane
like a meteorite of feathered rubbing,
beak and claw ensuring the whole room lifted an inch
before rushing to the window,
now flecked with crimson loss and hairline fractures,
a scream trapped tight behind the teeth of a child.

poetry for pablo

at that age i was summoned

abruptly
it touched me

violent ...

i was without
words

i was without
winter fires

it touched me
and
poetry arrived.

burning, burning

there are times when i can taste my heartbeat
i can feel
my blood *slipping through* my ecstatic veins as it
rushes from my brain to my bones to the
beautiful stars
and it is cold out tonight but i feel like the eyes
of god are
burning, burning
a hole into my needs and desires and
he sees what it is that my soul thirsts for
and it is to *walk backwards into the sweet*
blue ocean.

heavy shelling

the pathway to the red front door
of number twenty two was bordered by two
immaculate waist high hedges parallel laurels
clipped and choked by a mothers pride
a post downfall nirvana for slugs and snails of all kinds
fat umber leopards mingled with aspersa and pomatia
leaving the route to the house a pyrrhic battleground
the cost of a war between giants and gastropods
tattered doc martens and crisp, cornflake shells
the sweet amber days were mere skirmishes
practice runs for the jet black midnight crusades
a sherry addled teenager hell bent on terror
full of repressed rage and egg shell anxiety
the snap, crackle and pop
the rustle and the razing
they never stood a chance
each step extinguishing life
each cut and thrust
dismantled the defences
until the red door
was cold breath close

voyage au bout de la nuit

"that is perhaps what we seek throughout life,
that and nothing more,
the greatest possible sorrow so as to become fully ourselves
before dying."

i was reading celine when they told me you'd died
a smokeless explosion of lactic acid and the old enemy
they said you'd made a sound not unlike a exhausted filament
popping and fizzing into the night on a black tidal wave of irres-
olution

"you can lose your way groping among the shadows of the past."

it seemed fitting that you'd lent me the book by which you lived
and i'd read it while you were dying
a cold old bitch until the very end, an alien in your own home

"the sadness of the world has different ways of getting to people
but it seems to succeed almost every time."

i got into the car and drove
there would be no one by your side
but i knew you'd be smiling

gecko

i had never been to a birthday party before
and really i had never seen how other people lived
so when we pulled up to this enormous house
and dara ran outside i just laughed and then
his mum took my coat and his dad gave me pop
then we played games and sang songs and later
on he showed me his present and it was a gecko
which is a type of lizard but i didn't think anyone
would ever get a real lizard for their birthday so
when he handed it to me i thought it was plastic
and threw it up in the air and it landed with a damp
pink thud that told me it was time to go home.

diner

if you walk past the diner just after seven o'clock
once dusk has bruised the pink peach flesh of the day
and the taxi lights scream yellow murders outside the window
you can see the waitress, now a cleaner, in her lime green smock,
whirling and pirouetting through the air with her mop,
a noble gas, a neon sign, dancing, slipping and scything
through the empty spaces,
fly free sweet jane doe

running, running

and gaia spake in howls and hell-noises
and from her vaginal teeth did drop a shimmering homunculus,
falling stone cold dead-drop towards the fearful plains running
running.
and as it hit the ground, the homunculus burnt the forests and
the hills
and the rivers running blue
and as it met a glistening foetus in the meadow of fruit,
the homunculus did gnash and gnaw and destroy the rivers run-
ning red
and as it met the animals and the trees and the flowers of the
land,
the homunculus did rape and raze and ejaculate into
the bleeding bodies of the garden running scared and as it spent
its life and lie
with the taste of foul shit stink wafting through its swollen aorta,
the homunculus turned to gaia and forced itself upon her,
tearing dead flesh flora from lifeless fauna running running.
and gaia did weep and woe and the earth was full of blood.

quim

and now that the nursery
has burnt crisp,
on junkyard nights we pick sides,
reach through mist and blood red scarves
and pull out the vertebrae of our
dog-limp marriage from
the abandoned salamander
skin that lies on the floor,
like a robe quick sharp flicked
from a shaking, sopping frame,
a quivering quim and a
welcoming cunt.

maps

1.
its nine thirty and i am at school and
we are outside on a warm day and
its the first time i appreciate the
shorts they make us wear because
my legs are warm and my arms are
warm and guy taylor and me are
walking past the playground area
towards the beautiful woods that
we are warned about at the start
of each term but we can't resist
because the trees look like broccoli
and the sun shatters into a million
tiny pins pricking the soft earth
floor because the leaves are real
thick like fur on bone and guy and
me don't talk we never do we just
walk towards the forbidden fruit our
own garden of eden and as we near
the woods we turn to each other and
smile and he takes my hand and i am
thirteen but this feels so natural that i
could be thirty nine and i would still
be as excited and happy as i am now.

2.
once we are inside the woods we
have nothing to fear and the school
yard is so far away it may as well be
on the moon and the cries and shouts
of the children sound like a television
turned all the way down and we grip
each other's hands tightly and i can

feel his palm is clammy and that makes
me even happier because mine is too.

3.
its dark now and we have been here for
ten minutes just walking and touching
and smiling and laughing and it feels
like just a second has passed but we both
know soon it will be time to go and rejoin
our classes and pretend that we are really
interested in maths and art and swimming
and learning and really all we care about is
each other and the forest and those moments
when we can stop pretending and just be who
we are among the trees and the pins and the
flashes of light so bright you can taste them
with your tongue and the smell of the earth
and feeling of relief and i never want
to leave but then it is time to leave so we do.

4.
the last time i saw guy taylor was yesterday
and my teacher says i will never see him again
and if i am lucky i will be let back into school
but by god if i ever so much as touch anyone
he will throw me out and my mum is sad and
my dad is sad and i am sad because i do not
know if guy is sad and the thought of never
seeing him again makes my stomach turn
over and i didn't even get a chance to say
goodbye or good luck or thank you or i
love you or hold him just one last time and
tell him that everything will be fine and not
to worry about who he is because he is a
walk in the fresh snow and a deep blue sky
and a night spent inside listening to the rain.

celestial frottage

amongst the magnificent husky trunks were ferns so feathered
they seemed to exist
only in theory. we picked buttery chanterelles, trompette de la
mort and amethyst deceivers.
elf cups and slippery jacks. i lit a fire and fried them in salted
butter and wild garlic,
the smells mingling with the cloying scent of charcoal.
as the light died the woods changed, from stained glass cathedral
to hushed intonation.
later my fingers found their way into you,
and amongst the celestial frottage of midnight in the forest,
we spoke in whispers.
before i lay with you i burnt the map in the dying clinkers of
the fire.

milk

last week a milk truck overturned on the motorway
causing several fatalities and dozens of casualties
and we drove past the stretch of road about twenty
minutes after it happened and saw the bodies laid
out and the cars crushed and the lorry driver
whimpering
and the mothers crying and the paramedics terrible
frantic as people died in their arms and the milk
was everywhere drying in the sun and mixing
with the blood they hadn't mopped up yet and
everything was a paler shade of what it had been before
but all i could think about was how much it stank.

fire

i love my sister she smells of rain and when she lies
next to me the fire
paints red and orange on her lips and skin
and daddy told me never to come back here
she takes me for walks to the shops and when i cry at
night
she gives me my teddy and slides in next to me and
her hair
smells like clean bedding and shampoo
i am crying and i try to stop
and my sister smells like rain
we never see mummy so when i cry my sister
gives me my teddy and tells me everything is going to
be alright
and she slides in to bed next to me and the fire
paints autumn on her
skin
and daddy put me in the back of a taxi cab and told
the driver to take
me
where they could help me
and my sister smells like rain
she helps me do my laces and talk to god and wash
my hands
and when she sits by the fire the flames paint her
pretty face
with flowers and flames and she smells like rain when
she slips in to
bed beside me
and she is crying and i am not crying
and she smells like fire and her face looks like rain
and daddy tells me never to come back again my sister is crying
and the rain looks like fire and i am crying because

my sister is not
crying anymore
and the fire paints her cheeks with flames and the
fire is out in my heart
and i am crying but my sister is not crying because
she is in bed beside
me
and daddy comes and tells me i can never come back
here
and my sisters fire has gone out
and the rain paints my face with tears
and i am going to a strange place
and i cannot sleep
and no one is here to slide into bed next to me
or give me my teddy.

i'm aging like everyone else

there is space in my life to regret my youth
now that the crushing inevitability of aphasia
and oxalis have smothered me like so many
great paintings choked so many great artists,
the canvas and acrylic combining to push drunk
love on whoever it was that woke up one night
with a silent scream, meringue like sheets damp
with sweat and poured viscid crimson paint into
the hole they never knew they were falling down.

stripes

the sun shits out
another day
as i wake up like a sine wave
pour through cream cotton sheets
a man made of yellowing organs
sleeps under a fed-ex van
with a plastic cup and a scuffed knee

check the exhausted chameleon
exploding with confetti as he
reaches the end of the zebra crossing
sings
this is life-
this is life-
-ah well-

psalm45/instafuck (words from psalm 45 + insta-fuck email advert)

hello sweetie i will blow you in the movie theatre
gird your sword!
let the king be enthralled by your beauty;
you are better to hurry rape me in my holes
in the movie theatre - honor him, for he is your lord.
i want you to dive in my soul as deep as it is possible
come and be inside of me...
...as deep as it is possible
gird your sword on your side...
...as deep as it is possible
 my heart is stirred by a noble theme...
...you got a sexy body!
i will show you what you would like to touch
i will perpetuate your memory through all generations;
people of wealth will seek your favor
come and be inside of me
i need a passionate mature man
don't forget me
fulfill my dream.

ode to a hooker

smoking a limp dick cigarette her silk gown
draped like sapphire mist on a
skeletal frame cacophonous birds
on her knees and shoulders flit and flutter
white hair thick with flake memories
of far off jacarandas her skin blistered
and peeled with gold leaf botox
and jet black crow trails
she opens her mouth and lays the red carpet

my brother and i

since my brother and i
sit stitching wings
onto butterflies

cross stitch
knit one
pearl one

release from the jar
we speak not
of family matters
of trivial demeanours
like our mother
lying in effluence
while my father
unravels like a spool of thread
we speak not

of the debt
the dogma
the destruction of
our beautiful wives
since my brother and i
create sweet music with
each other's ribcages
like flesh and form
snuff boxed silhouette
black crow dreamscapes
we daren't speak
of little boy blue
deciduous trees

death incarnate
and the rattle and hum
of our mothers
bronchial fire
since my brother and i
lay still inside one another
acid reflux and shameful glances
boiled sweet reflections
mist eye menders
hospital trolleys ambushed
sent back to whence they came
we do not have time
for trivialities
such as life
death
and the flames that lick
suck and caress
at our parents ethereal chaos
since my brother and i
plough fields of youthful ambivalence
with rusted tractor wheels
and rabbits slit from ear
to twitching ear
we do not have time
to discuss the cancer
or the amputation of limbs
the war in the east
or the son in the west
since my brother and i
live only for ourselves
we do not have time
to attend funerals
and light pyres
for those we love
and those we lost
while we were trading places
and melting like wax
into the eyes of eternity.

from shard;

 rust:rothko

the view from my window which
takes in blossom, willow and rose
each of many colour each of many texture
now wafer dull like rothko
rust on a tin can rust in my mind

from shard;

strobe(a haiku)

s/e/e/n/t/h/r/o/u/g/h/a/s/t/r/o/b/e/l/i/g/h/t
p/e/o/p/l/e/m/o/v/e/i/n/s/l/o/w/m/o/t/i/o/n
c/u/t/l/o/o/s/e/f/r/o/m/t/i/m/e/s/c/h/a/i/n/s

from shard;

16 words for cold

cold,
kalt, koud, kűlm
kylmä, kubanda, koue,
kadhemen froid, frío, freddo, fred
hladno, hladan, fret
hotze

les bulot

in my dream i am back at les bulot
cautiously trawling the fish soup
afraid of probing its depths and
finding myself hopelessly out of
my comfort zone wishing i had
opted for the sirloin steak
which you were now pushing
around your plate with the silver
cutlery making blood and cream and
the lissom pomme-frite mingle
sensually on the bone china plate
and now you are laughing at me
because i have found sand in
the bottom of the bowl and you
say that it shows it is authentic and
i push the bowl aside and sip the
wine and breathe in the salty air
and suddenly i am aware that this
is a dream and my heart breaks a
little inside as it does each time
i leave les bulot and return to
the stark fire i now inhabit alone.

naked

its raining pellets so i dash home as fast as i can
and at the door i take off my coat and shoes
and then i take off my top and jeans and then
i peel off my sopping wet skin and shed my
withered muscles and eggshell bones
until i am just a huge pile of clotting blood and
a bright blue soul, the brightest blue, and i
ask you now what more can i do?

fante/pollock

its cold , cold beyond the walled garden
both the literal one outside my house
and the metaphorical one in my mind,
our minds where the cranial nerves and
the butter yellow of the creeping wisteria
mingle in the ever fading dusk-light of the
nebulous yawn of time and now i'm standing
in a field talking to you about john fante
and now i'm sitting by your chair as you die
and now neither of us have even been born
yet and the gluons and the quarks and the
electrons splatter against the cosmic wall
like a jackson pollock forged by god.

dog

there is a dog at the end of the lane
who tells me he is the reincarnation
of a thirteen year old girl who shot
her face into compass points rather
than deal with her dads tricky fingers
and sometimes i sit in the bright pink
sunset and stroke the beautiful dog
but sometimes i do not.

river

today i played joni mitchell's 'blue' backwards
expecting to hear the devil
but instead causing time and matter to condense and
reverse
thus causing considerable change within myself and
the universe
butterflies began stitching themselves into cocoons
as my eyeballs melted and ran like tears down my
cheeks
the screams of a thousand lost souls were swallowed
and choked on
and spat out again
my teeth pushed back through my gums and burst
out the gelatinous
mess
that once was my face
millions of bullets returned to millions of guns like
faithful dogs
the sky turned green and the grass turned blue
every musical note returned to its instrument
every thought turned to a silent whisper
and every human being turned into a glint in no one's
eye
from my vantage point
as a puddle on the floor of eternity
i briefly spotted richard dawkins crying into his teacup
before he too melted and i absorbed him
through spiritual osmosis.

birth

from his lank hair fell a swarm of jet black locusts
and he cried and he cried and as his sparkling fish-tears hit the
ground
they sent yellow gorse and desolate willow punching
through the baked
red earth
and his silent scream sent teeth tumbling from his
mouth crashing upon
the dying soil
like meteors or monoliths and he showed me his
wrists and cut into each
one with sickening clarity
was a message;

it is time.

nerium

the path to your door was lined
on either side by oleander bushes
that you had planted to keep
everyone away and it had worked
because it was three weeks before
they found you sitting in your chair
disintegrating and dressed in the
violet smock i had brought you
the last time i visited the house.
i read just the other day that the
scientific community had attempted to
use oleander extract to cure cancer
but it hadn't worked.

library

nursing the oily spawn in your belly with
smoky cups of lapsang souchon you
let slip a pillow-sigh as you closed
the book and, with a permanent marker,
scrawled 'these are not the words that
make it better' onto the cover before
casting the book into the mouth of
the seething fire as if it were tinder.

s.a.d light

you are like january when you come over
and you cry so much your tears saturate
the ground and the mud and the root balls
of great trees like gargantuan florets of aging broccoli
bringing them crashing down in a death metal drum roll.
i turn on the s.a.d light but the bulb is broken
and it dies like everything must with a faceless pop
so you leave and from my window
i see the great big sky and its is falling,
falling just for you

gingko

carefully i place your ashes in a biodegradable urn
poking a hole like a lunar crater with my trembling
forefinger i carefully slip a pale white ginkgo seed
amidst the charred remains as you had asked me in
tumescent whispers on your final night on earth.
i place the urn on the cruddy windowsill, where the
fugacious sun-beams and my forgetful watering
caused you to grow, in time, i
nto a beautiful biloba tree.
you stayed for a brief time in the kitchen
but then moved to the garden where you prospered
and eventually, thirty painful years of dust and disease later
you grew strong enough for the second part of your dream
to come true and this morning i hung myself
from your sturdiest branch
and now we are together in light, boundless and abiding,
timeless, termless and free.

absinthe makes the heart grow fonder

sometimes i stare
at the enamelled absinthe poster
we bought from a thrift store in montmartre
an overpriced attempt
to become more cultured
i look at the lady
in her green dress
and her green hat
pouring green liquor
into emíle cohl's cup
and i remember
the night before we bought it
we sat up all night
in the cemetery where dumas was buried
(i had to tell you who he was)
and we drank from a bottle
of pale green absinthe
and convinced ourselves
we were hallucinating
(though they stopped putting wormwood in years ago)
desperate to feel
to mean
something more
than just bones
more than just an enamelled sign
and a return ticket home

forks

fingers splayed,
copper conducts

lightning, shoots
savage forks

down clenched
fists and rigid

limbs as pulsing,
panting, power-

less we fuse
together and

filaments sizzle
in sweet spring bulbs.

god/godot

i lie in a field and speak to god/godot about the
click clack asphyxiation cut throat cash flow
scarlet shame when each day dark side death
shadows and suicide note sunbeams wish wash
over my face paint hope and hatred i fly i lie i
cry hoarse please get me off this shit shot fucked
up ball of spinning hatred and insanity fuelled by
turpentine dreams and fat cat green chasing rapists
who unpick the seams of leather bound nightmares
with his story told by a million screaming children
coated black ash tar pit bones of ancient beings
ground down to memory found to replicate the
mistakes made by our mothers picking apples and
stitches while we fawn over child porn and vapidity
caustic he screams at my psilocybin kid thoughts
light bulb notions fold me in two as weeping
earth washes away the nicotine stain burnt hair
smell of monopoly and biology, a dichotomy of
rotting leaves and linoleum garbage smoke then
skeletal trees punch forth from ashen lands reek
of he and thee no fear for life no fear for him
just pity and third reich leather belt strapped
tight around the arm of gaia spat on shot up with
fifty seven varieties of special sauce.
clouds of burnt flesh cherish the choice of one
last night as the penumbra of god/godot casts half cut
chain shots across my tallow skin silken fog forces
me to my knees before tightrope holocaust cancer
ward despair fucks deep his might strikes the chord
flies the flag while we hunt for opals in the dusk
of time and then the clock strikes and i wake.

manifesto

take drugs and
fuck girls
because nothing is waiting for you
except worms and
trees and the
deepest blue sky

quantum

the single best
day of my life was when
i read a book about quantum
theory and it said that everything
that can happen will happen and that
there are infinite universes with infinite me's
and infinite you's and infinite colours and infinite
feelings and to me that was the greatest thing that ever
happened because if there is just one single universe in which
we are happy together and holding hands and lying in purple
grass
then i am willing to put up with the infinite other universes
where we
are not

l.o.v.e

that night we both dreamt of resurrection

i roll your emotions like a rubber ball between my glowing palms
and take your minds yolk in my veins

you whispered *its so brittle, this life*
you were uncontrollably sad trembling
because we will never be able to occupy
the exact same physical space.

i stand before a crowd and read poetry
but i cannot pronounce the word *love*

6.7.45

the stuff gathering
inexorably on our
shelves is just bits
of you and me
and the cats

at worlds end

perennial subservience
has led to
poundland prayers
and
teeth spat
across
school-
yards.
i spend my
days waiting
for night
and
my nights in
a daze.
it is two thousand and sixteen and i do not know anyone who
isn't

terrified.

cryptic (text taken from times cryptic crossword)

oh, very sad
we cut and ran

looking fit   losing wings
looking fit   losing wings
nothing like slender girls
fast food returned
slender girls
funny girl with wig
funny girls
returned
sad
we cut
and ran
basic stripping caught in the act (like macbeth) caught in the act
model turning on model
half unbuttoned in the act
model turning on model
half unbuttoned in the act
model turning on model
half unbuttoned in the act
          oral sex   oral sex
upset about blundering courage

cut and ran (like macbeth)
nervous
showed signs of inflation

fast food!?!

girls
      showed signs of inflation

oral sex
     giving head in the morning
oral sex

looking fit losing wings
(we cut and ran)
finally switched off.

blusher

discount blusher
only covers
half the bruises

casually discussing the infinite

we are all brittle and spotless and so infinite
standing under the same endless spark blue sky
staring through the generations of madness
to find a reason for this seeming insignificance
and god is not the reason but man is the reason
man and his eternal need to cause suffering to
those who deserve better and now i ask of you
to shed your life and shed your light and join me
in the beautiful, noble race for death through
peace and whispers and lord let the electrons
flow through my fingers as i kiss your cheek.

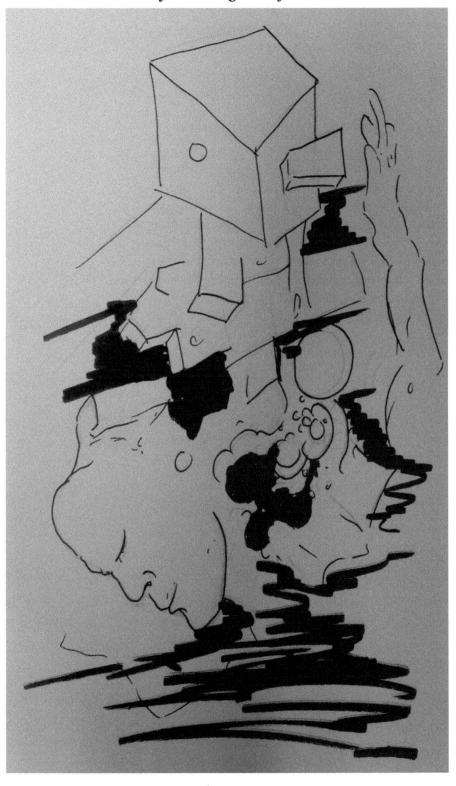